WORLD HERITAGE

Protecting Human Masterpieces

Brendan and Debbie Gallagher

Smart Apple Media
P.O. Box 3263
Mankato, MN, 56002

First published in 2010 by
MACMILLAN EDUCATION AUSTRALIA PTY LTD
15–19 Claremont St, South Yarra, Australia 3141

Visit our web site at www.macmillan.com.au or go directly to www.macmillanlibrary.com.au

Associated companies and representatives throughout the world.

Copyright © Brendan and Debbie Gallagher 2010

Library of Congress Cataloging-in-Publication Data

Gallagher, Brendan.
    Protecting human masterpieces / Brendan and Debbie Gallagher.
       p. cm. — (World Heritage)
    Includes index.
    ISBN 978-1-59920-580-9 (library bound)
    1. Architecture—Conservation and restoration—Juvenile literature. 2. Cultural property—Protection—Juvenile literature. 3. World Heritage areas—Juvenile literature. I. Gallagher, Debbie, 1969– II. Title.
    NA105.G35 2011
    363.6'9—dc22
                                2009053011

Publisher: Carmel Heron
Managing Editor: Vanessa Lanaway
Editor: Kirstie Innes-Will
Proofreader: Paige Amor
Designer: Kerri Wilson
Page layout: Kerri Wilson
Photo researcher: Legend Images
Illustrator: Guy Holt
Production Controller: Vanessa Johnson

Manufactured in China by Macmillan Production (Asia) Ltd.
Kwun Tong, Kowloon, Hong Kong
Supplier Code: CP December 2009

Acknowledgments
The author and the publisher are grateful to the following for permission to reproduce copyright material:

Cover photograph of the Great Wall of China at Mutianyu © Anna Nemkovich/Shutterstock

Photographs courtesy of:
© Bayon/Dreamstime.com, 24; © Gbond/Dreamstime.com, 28; © Holgs/Dreamstime.com, 18; © Phillip Minnis/Dreamstime.com, 22; © Herbert Eisengruber/fotolia, 21; Matt Cardy/Getty Images, 23; Larry Dale Gordon/Getty Images, 31; Kenneth Garrett/Getty Images, 30; © Adivin/iStockphoto, 8; © John Carnemolla/iStockphoto, 15; © Gueorgui Ianakiev/iStockphoto, 16; Petra National Trust, 19; Photolibrary/Jose Fuste Raga, 25; Photolibrary/Govin-Sorel , 17; Photolibrary/Ted Mead, 14; Picture Media/Reuters/Manuel Silvestri, 29; Shutterstock, 26, 27; © Evangelos/Shutterstock, 6; © Jarno Gonzalez Zarraonandia/Shutterstock, 13; © Andrey Grinyov/Shutterstock, 7; © Vladimir Korostyshevskiy/Shutterstock, 10; © Luciano Mortula/Shutterstock, 11; © Anna Nemkovich/Shutterstock, 1; © VanHart/Shutterstock, 9; © vincent369/Shutterstock, 12; © Peter von Bucher/Shutterstock, 20.

Please note
At the time of printing, the Internet addresses appearing in this book were correct. Owing to the dynamic nature of the Internet, however, we cannot guarantee that all these addresses will remain correct.

Contents

When a word in the text is printed in **bold**, look for its meaning in the glossary boxes.

World Heritage

There are places around the world that are important to all peoples. We call these places the world's heritage. Some of these places are human creations, such as the pyramids of Egypt. Some are natural creations, such as the Great Barrier Reef of Australia.

The World Heritage List

The World Heritage List is a list of **sites** that must be protected because they have some kind of outstanding importance for the world. This list was created in 1972, and new places are added every year. Each site on the World Heritage List belongs to one of the following categories:

 NATURAL – for example, waterfalls, forests, or deserts

 CULTURAL – for example, a building or a site where an event occurred

 MIXED – if it has both natural and cultural features

UNESCO

UNESCO, the United Nations Educational, Scientific, and Cultural Organization, is the organization that maintains the World Heritage List. Find out more at www.unesco.org.

World Heritage Criteria

A place can be **inscribed** on the World Heritage List if it meets at least one of these ten **criteria**, and is an outstanding example of it. The criteria are:

 i a masterpiece of human creative genius

 ii a site representing the sharing of human ideas

 iii a site representing a special culture or civilization

 iv a historical building or landscape from a period of history

 v a site representing or important to a traditional culture

 vi a site representing an important event, idea, living tradition, or belief

 vii a very beautiful or unique natural site

 viii a site showing evidence of Earth's history

 ix an important ecosystem

 x an important natural habitat for species protection

KEY TERMS

sites	places
inscribed	added to
criteria	rules or requirements

Protecting Human Masterpieces

Protecting Human Masterpieces is about protecting the most amazing places on Earth created by humans. These are places where examples of human creative **genius** can be found. The genius may be that of a particular person or of a whole **civilization**.

Criteria for Protecting Human Masterpieces

Many of the places in this book are important for many reasons. This book focuses on just one reason: how a place is a **masterpiece** or shows human genius. This is reason i on the list of criteria for being on the World Heritage List.

Protecting World Heritage

Governments around the world have all agreed to protect the sites on the World Heritage List. A site that is not being properly looked after may be put on the List of World Heritage in Danger. See http://whc.unesco.org/en/158/

This map shows the location of the World Heritage sites covered in this book.

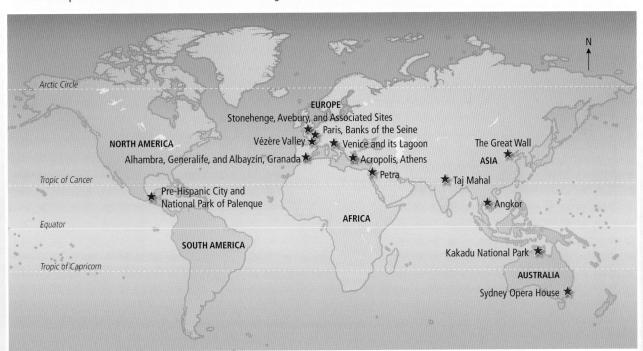

genius   extraordinary ability in a subject or activity

civilization   the culture and society of a particular group in history

masterpiece   an amazing or masterful creation

Acropolis, Athens

The Acropolis is a collection of ancient buildings on a rocky hill overlooking Athens, Greece. Its most important buildings were built in the 400s B.C.. They have inspired people throughout history with their beauty and style.

FACT FILE

GREECE

The Acropolis protects examples of the creative genius of the Ancient Greeks.

Category:

Criteria:

The Ancient Greeks designed the buildings of the Acropolis with perfect balance, blending them with the natural landscape.

the Parthenon

the Acropolis rock

other ancient buildings

TIMELINE

400s B.C.	447–432 B.C.	A.D. 1806	1987
The Ancient Greeks organise a large building project on the Acropolis.	The Parthenon is built.	Lord Thomas Elgin removes Greek art from the Acropolis and sends it to England.	The Acropolis is inscribed on the World Heritage List.

Reliefs were cut away from the wall above the pillars of the Parthenon.

Important Features

The Ancient Greeks placed large columns at the entrances to their buildings and they decorated them with sculptures. The Parthenon, a temple dedicated to the goddess Athena, had 92 marble **reliefs** along the outside walls. The reliefs show scenes from Greek myths and wars. The Parthenon is one of the greatest building achievements of Ancient Athens.

Did You Know?

In 1687, the Parthenon was badly damaged when a ship from Venice, Italy, fired a cannon at it.

Issues

Lord Thomas Elgin removed some sculptures from the Acropolis, including 15 of the Parthenon's reliefs. He later sold them to the British government, which passed them on to the British Museum. Today, the Greek government would like to see the sculptures returned to Athens to be **preserved** in the Acropolis Museum.

GLOSSARY

reliefs   sculptures carved on walls
preserved   protected or kept safe

Alhambra, Generalife, and Albayzín, Granada

The Alhambra, Generalife, and Albayzín are three parts of the **medieval** city of Granada, Spain. The Alhambra is a fortress and a palace on a hill. On another hill is the Generalife, a summer palace for the city's rulers. The Albayzín was the main part of the city. Both the Alhambra and the gardens of the Generalife are extraordinary works of art. They were built by Islamic Arabs from North Africa, called Moors, who lived in Spain for over 700 years.

FACT FILE

SPAIN

The Alhambra and Generalife are masterpieces, examples of the creative genius of the Moors.

Category:

Criteria:

The Alhambra was built above the surrounding area to protect it from attack.

later Christian palace

red fortress

palaces of the Alhambra

TIMELINE

700s	1234	1302–09	1492	1984	1994
The Moors conquer most of modern Spain and Portugal.	The building of the Alhambra begins.	The Generalife palace and gardens are built.	Control of Granada passes from the Moors to Christian rulers.	The Alhambra and Generalife are inscribed on the World Heritage List.	Albayzín is added to the listing.

Important Features

The Moors decorated the walls and ceilings of the Alhambra palace with lines and circles, creating beautiful shapes and patterns. The word *Alhambra* comes from the Arabic words for "red fortress." The palace was built from red clay found in the surrounding area.

Issues

The site is not facing any serious threats and **conservationists** restore the artworks carefully. The Fountain of the Lions was damaged over time from extreme weather conditions and poor-quality water running through it. The court where the fountain sits was closed to allow restoration work to be carried out.

Did You Know?

The words "There is no victor but Allah" are inscribed hundreds of times on the walls, columns, and arches of the Alhambra.

The room called the Lookout Place of the Queen is considered one of the most beautiful in the Alhambra.

GLOSSARY

medieval	from the Middle Ages, A.D. 400–1500
conservationists	people who protect an area

Angkor

Angkor is an area of temples, monuments, and water features in Cambodia. The area was the center of the Khmer **Empire** between A.D. 900 and 150. The Khmer are the people of this region. The most important of the temples is Angkor Wat.

The magnificent temple complex of Angkor Wat has become a symbol of Cambodia.

five central towers

Angkor Wat

moat

TIMELINE

800	1113–1150	1992	2004
The Khmer establish Angkor as the center of their empire.	Angkor Wat is built.	Angkor is inscribed on the World Heritage List and then added to the List of World Heritage in Danger.	Angkor is removed from the List of World Heritage in Danger.

Angkor Wat is covered with beautiful engravings and other artworks, which show the genius of the Khmer.

Important Features

Angkor Wat was designed as a temple mountain, with the central towers representing the home of the gods. Besides the temple itself, many of the works of art at Angkor Wat are masterpieces. The Khmer sculpted images of their gods, showing them in graceful positions. The skill needed to create these sculptures and other works of art shows the genius of the Khmer.

Issues

Angkor was added to the List of World Heritage in Danger because it had little protection. Some temples were close to falling down and tourists were removing parts of the temples. **Landmines** had been left on the site from the Cambodian Civil War. Efforts have now been made to protect the buildings and the area has been removed from the list.

Did You Know?

Angkor was once a city covering the same area as modern Los Angeles.

GLOSSARY

empire	a group of nations and kingdoms with one ruler
landmines	buried explosives

The Great Wall

The Great Wall is a series of walls that are about 3,510 miles (5,650 kilometers) in length in northern China. It stretches over plains, deserts, and mountains. The Great Wall is a masterpiece of human building and a treasure of the Chinese people.

FACT FILE

CHINA

The Great Wall protects the creative genius of many **dynasties** of the Chinese **Empire**.

Category:

Criteria:

mountains

The Great Wall

tower

This section, Jinshanling, is one of the most beautiful parts of the Great Wall.

TIMELINE

400s B.C.	Around 220 B.C.	A.D. 1368–1644	1987
The Chinese start building walls to protect their northern borders from invasion.	The **emperor** Qin Shi Huang connects different defensive walls to create a great wall.	The Great Wall becomes the world's largest military structure during the Ming dynasty.	The Great Wall is inscribed on the World Heritage List.

Important Features

The Great Wall was built, rebuilt, and maintained over many centuries. It was during the Ming dynasty, A.D. 1368–1644, that it truly became a masterpiece. The Chinese built thousands of miles of wall using incredibly well-matched bricks. The Great Wall is a masterpiece because of the perfection of its building and the way it blends into its surroundings.

Issues

In many places the Great Wall is crumbling. Local people use the stones for their own purposes. Tourists remove parts as souvenirs. Without **conservation**, natural forces will **erode** the wall. As much as two thirds of it may already be damaged or destroyed.

The length of the Great Wall makes it very hard to protect, and many parts are crumbling.

Did You Know?
It is often claimed that the Great Wall is visible to human eyes from space, but this is not true.

GLOSSARY

dynasties	sequences of rulers from the same family
empire	a group of nations and kingdoms with one ruler
emperor	the ruler of an empire
conservation	protection or restoration from damage or loss
erode	wear away

Kakadu National Park

Kakadu National Park is an area of wetlands, flood plains, woodlands, and **rain forests** in northern Australia. Kakadu is the home of different **Indigenous Australian peoples.** Their artwork, drawn over thousands of years, is found in caves and on rocks throughout the park.

There are three main rock art sites at Nourlangie Rock, part of Kakadu National Park.

FACT FILE

AUSTRALIA

Kakadu National Park protects the creative genius of Indigenous Australian rock art.

Category:

Criteria:

Nourlangie Rock

TIMELINE

50,000 years ago	18,000 years ago	1981	1992
Indigenous Australians arrive in the Kakadu area.	The oldest rock art still surviving in Kakadu is drawn.	Kakadu National Park is inscribed on the World Heritage List.	Cultural values are added to the inscription for Kakadu National Park.

Important Features

The great variety of rock art in Kakadu tells us about the Indigenous Australians who have been living in the area for tens of thousands of years. Some of the artwork shows legendary heroes and **ancestors**. Other artwork, called "X ray style," shows the inside organs and bones of animals. While the last rock painting in Kakadu was completed in 1986, local Indigenous Australians continue to paint on paper, bark, and other materials.

This example of X ray style rock art shows, at the top, Namondjok, a creation ancestor.

Issues

Much of the rock art in Kakadu is found in areas sheltered from rain and sun. However, **introduced species** such as pigs and buffalo use these areas for shelter. The animals can damage the art by rubbing against the rock. Park managers are trying to remove these species from Kakadu.

Did You Know?

There are at least 3,000 rock art sites in Kakadu. Some estimates say there may be as many as 15,000.

GLOSSARY

rain forests	forests that receive a lot of rainfall
Indigenous Australian peoples	the first people to live in Australia
ancestors	people who came before you in your family
introduced species	plants or animals that are not native to an area

Paris, Banks of the Seine

Paris, Banks of the Seine includes the buildings along the Seine River of Paris, France. It stretches from the Île Saint Louis that sits in the middle of the Seine River to the Eiffel Tower, about 4 miles (6 kilometers) to the west. The Eiffel Tower, named after its creator Gustave Eiffel, is the most well-known of Paris's masterpieces.

FACT FILE

FRANCE

Paris, Banks of the Seine protects many examples of creative genius, including the Eiffel Tower.

Category: ✋

Criteria: 🗿 🔄

🏛

The Eiffel Tower is one of the most famous buildings in the world.

Eiffel Tower

Seine River

TIMELINE

250 B.C.	A.D. 1887–89	1991
The Parisii peoples settle on the banks of the Seine.	The Eiffel Tower is built for the 1889 International Exhibition of Paris.	Paris, Banks of the Seine is inscribed on the World Heritage List.

Important Features

When the Eiffel Tower was completed in 1889, it was the tallest building in the world. It continues to be the tallest structure in Paris at 1,062 feet (324 meters). Eiffel wanted the tower to show beauty and strength. Many people hated the tower at first but it has since become a symbol of Paris and the French people.

Issues

The buildings of Paris, Banks of the Seine are well maintained. To keep the Eiffel Tower's appearance, it is painted every seven years. Pollution from traffic is a problem, but sections along the banks of the river are closed to traffic to reduce this problem.

A worker, high up on the Eiffel Tower, carries out maintenance work to look after the tower.

Petra

Petra in Jordan is an ancient city carved from sandstone rock in a desert landscape surrounded by mountains. The city was the capital of the Nabataeans, Arabic peoples from the region, in the 100s B.C.. UNESCO considers Petra to be one of the world's most precious cultural sites.

FACT FILE

Petra protects the many works of art that the Nabataeans carved out of the sandstone.

Category:

Criteria:

sandstone rock

carved features

Al Khazneh

The Treasury Building, known in Arabic as Al Khazneh, is one of Petra's works of art.

TIMELINE

100s B.C.	A.D. 168–106	106	1985
Petra is built as the capital of the Nabataean kingdom.	At the height of the kingdom, 30,000 people live in Petra.	The Roman **emperor** claims Petra and the Nabataean kingdom.	Petra is inscribed on the World Heritage List.

Important Features

The Nabataeans were traders in spices and perfumes. The money they gained from trade allowed them to employ architects and builders to create the works at Petra. The Nabataeans used hammers and chisels to carve approximately 3,000 homes, banquet halls, **sacred** areas, and tombs out of the sandstone.

Did You Know?

To enter Petra visitors need to walk through a **canyon** 0.6 miles (1 kilometer) long, with walls 262 feet (80 meters) thick on each side.

Issues

Many of the caves inside Petra were once used for ordinary purposes, such as storage or keeping animals. The caves were also used by people selling souvenirs or food. These uses were **eroding** the sandstone as well as spoiling the look of the site. However, many of the caves have now been emptied. There are further plans to stop these activities from affecting the masterpieces at Petra.

Eight of eleven restaurants in the caves at Petra have been closed to protect the area.

GLOSSARY

emperor	the ruler of an empire
sacred	holy, religious
canyon	a deep valley with steep sides
eroding	wearing away

Pre-Hispanic City and National Park of Palenque

The **Pre-Hispanic** City and National Park of Palenque is an ancient Mayan city located in the south of Mexico. The city, which is now in ruins, was lived in for about 600 years from A.D. 300 to 900.

FACT FILE

MEXICO

Palenque protects the creative genius – in architecture and artwork – of the Mayan civilization.

Category:

Criteria:

Temple of Inscriptions

palace

Palenque is an outstanding example of the best of Mayan creativity.

TIMELINE

100 B.C.	A.D. 500–700	900	1981	1987
People first live in the Palenque area.	The Mayan civilization reaches its peak at Palenque.	Only a small farming community remains at Palenque.	Palenque is made a national park.	Palenque is inscribed on the World Heritage List.

This mask was found on the body of a Mayan king in the Temple of Inscriptions at Palenque.

Important Features

Palenque was a small city but it contained about 1,500 structures. The Temple of Inscriptions is one of the most interesting buildings of Palenque. It was once decorated with designs of flowers and figures, painted in a vivid red color. The temple contained spectacular works of art. These, along with the carvings and sculptures throughout the ancient city, show that the Mayans were highly creative.

Did You Know?
A secret stairway inside the Temple of Insciptions leads to the tomb of Pakal the Great who ruled Palenque from A.D. 615 to 683.

Issues

The Pre-Hispanic City and National Park of Palenque is a well-protected area. Visitors are not allowed into certain areas so as to protect sensitive parts of the buildings. Visitors are also asked not to remove anything from the ancient city.

GLOSSARY

Pre-Hispanic   from the time before the Spanish conquered South and Central America in the 1500s

Stonehenge, Avebury, and Associated Sites

Stonehenge, Avebury, and Associated Sites are circles of stone **pillars** and other structures created in ancient times. These stone structures are outstanding creative achievements. The best known of these structures is Stonehenge. There is nothing like Stonehenge in the entire world. Stonehenge is the best known **prehistoric** monument in Europe.

FACT FILE

UNITED KINGDOM

Stonehenge, Avebury, and Associated Sites protects masterpieces created by the ancient peoples of England.

Category:

Criteria:

Stonehenge was built as a burial place, by farming communities, beginning about 3000 B.C..

lintel

stone pillars

megaliths

TIMELINE

3000 B.C.	A.D. 1920s	1977	1986	2007
Construction of Stonehenge begins.	Efforts are made to stop building and farms moving closer to Stonehenge.	Stonehenge is roped off and visitors are no longer permitted to walk among the stones.	The site is inscribed on the World Heritage List.	Plans to remove roads near Stonehenge are cancelled.

Important Features

The huge rocks at Stonehenge, called megaliths, once formed a full circle. The circle was made up of stone pillars with other large, curved rocks, called lintels, placed on the pillars. The builders of Stonehenge carved the stones to make them fit. For the time, the construction of Stonehenge was extraordinary.

Issues

A major road passes through the Stonehenge area. The road spoils the views of Stonehenge, but plans to run the road under the ground were canceled at the end of 2007 because of the cost involved.

Stonehenge is said to be one of the worst managed World Heritage sites in the United Kingdom.

GLOSSARY

pillars	tall posts or columns
prehistoric	from the time before writing was invented

Sydney Opera House

The Sydney Opera House is a performing arts center built on a stretch of land reaching into Sydney Harbour, Australia. It was designed by Danish architect Jørn Utzon. The builders of the Opera House showed great creativity in making such a difficult structure.

FACT FILE

AUSTRALIA

The Sydney Opera House protects a masterpiece of architecture, engineering, and sculpture.

Category:

Criteria:

The Sydney Opera House has become an icon of Australia.

Opera House

shells

massive platform

Sydney Harbour

TIMELINE

1956	1957	1973	2007
A competition is held to see who could come up with the best idea for an Opera House in Sydney – Jørn Utzon wins.	Construction of the Sydney Opera House begins.	The Sydney Opera House is completed.	Sydney Opera House is inscribed on the World Heritage List.

The steps leading up to the Sydney Opera House, called the Monumental Steps, are nearly 328 feet (100 meters) wide.

Important Features

The Opera House has three sets of giant shells fixed together on a massive platform. The steps running up to the entrance of the Opera House were inspired by Mayan building styles from Mexico. The setting of the building on a piece of land on Sydney Harbour is spectacular, and the Opera House is one of the greatest building works of the 1900s.

Issues

The Opera House is very well maintained. Jørn Utzon, the architect of the building, died in 2008, but any changes to the Opera House in the future will be based on his ideas.

Did You Know?

The Sydney Opera House has more than 1,000 rooms.

25

Taj Mahal

The Taj Mahal was built by the fifth ruler of the Mughal **Empire** of India, Shah Jahan, in memory of his wife, Queen Arjumand Banu Begam. It is made up of different buildings, each separate and yet all combining perfectly. The **symmetry** and balance of the buildings make the Taj Mahal a work of art.

FACT FILE

INDIA

The Taj Mahal protects the creative genius of Shah Jahan and the Mughal Empire.

Category:

Criteria:

The Taj Mahal houses the tombs of the Muslim Emperor of India Shah Jahan and his wife.

domes

minarets

arches

convex space

symmetry

TIMELINE

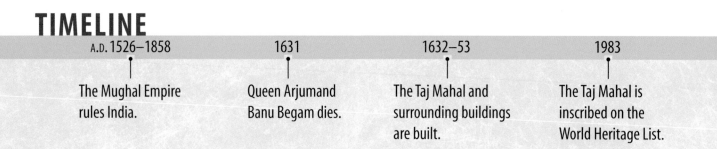

A.D. 1526–1858	1631	1632–53	1983
The Mughal Empire rules India.	Queen Arjumand Banu Begam dies.	The Taj Mahal and surrounding buildings are built.	The Taj Mahal is inscribed on the World Heritage List.

Important Features

The Taj Mahal is a funeral mosque. It is both a tomb for Queen Arjumand Banu Begam and a Muslim place of worship. The builders of the Taj Mahal used arches, domes, and convex spaces to create an inspiring effect. Inside, semi-precious and precious stones were used to create patterns of flowers and beautiful handwriting. The Taj Mahal is the greatest creation of Mughal architecture.

Issues

To protect the Taj Mahal and the areas around it, there are restrictions on building projects. For example, no shopping center can be built within 656 feet (200 meters) of the Taj Mahal area.

Did You Know?

About 20,000 workers were involved in the building of the Taj Mahal.

Words from the Muslim holy book, the Koran, are inscribed in Arabic on the walls of the Taj Mahal.

GLOSSARY

empire   a group of nations and kingdoms with one ruler
symmetry   having two halves or sides that are exactly the same

Venice and its Lagoon

Venice and its **Lagoon** is an area of **marshland** in Italy that is separated from the sea by a raised sandbank. By the 900s Venice was a powerful seaport. The city of Venice is built on 118 different islands. It is a unique artistic creation and its setting on water has inspired artists and writers for many centuries.

The Palazzo Santa Sofia is one of Venice's many masterpieces.

FACT FILE

Venice and its Lagoon protects the city of Venice, a masterpiece of architecture.

Category:

Criteria:

islands in the lagoon

Palazzo Santa Sofia

canals

TIMELINE

A.D. 400s	900s	1796	1987
Romans fleeing attacks by Germanic peoples move to the sandy islands of the Venice lagoon.	Venice becomes a major sea power.	Venice is taken over by the Austrian army, ending the city's independence.	Venice is inscribed on the World Heritage List.

Important Features

Not only is the overall city of Venice a masterpiece, but many of its buildings are also masterpieces. The Palazzo Santa Sofia, on the Grand Canal, is known as "the golden house" because of the detailed decorations on its front wall. Saint Mark's Basilica is the best known of Venice's churches and is sometimes called "the church of gold." Venice inspired many artists, including Tintoretto, who painted the walls and ceiling of the Scuola di San Rocco, a building in Venice.

Venice, including Saint Mark's square, was flooded in 2008. Flooding is a big threat to Venice.

Issues

The greatest threat facing Venice comes from the sea. The city has been flooded many times and with **global warming** leading to higher sea levels, the threat of flooding is even greater. Experts are working to instal a barrier system by 2012 that will protect Venice from rising sea levels.

Did You Know?
Food deliveries and emergency services use the canals to access different parts of the city.

GLOSSARY

lagoon	a shallow area of water cut off from the sea
marshland	a flooded grassy plain
global warming	increases in temperatures on Earth

Prehistoric Sites and Decorated Caves of the Vézère Valley

FACT FILE

FRANCE ★

The Prehistoric Sites and Decorated Caves of the Vézère Valley protect masterpieces of prehistoric art.

Category:

Criteria:

The Prehistoric Sites and Decorated Caves of the Vézère Valley, France, are places where **prehistoric** drawings and paintings are located. The drawings and paintings were created in the age known as the Stone Age. The people of the time were hunter gatherers. This means that they did not plant crops or raise animals, but instead hunted wild animals and ate berries and fruit.

limestone cliffs

Vézère River

Most of the prehistoric art is found in the limestone cliffs beside the Vézère River.

TIMELINE

15,000–10,000 B.C.	A.D. 1940	1963	1979	1983
Ancient peoples decorate the sites and caves of the Vézère Valley.	The Lascaux Cave is discovered by four teenagers.	The Lascaux Cave is closed to the public.	The site is inscribed on the World Heritage List.	A replica of the Lascaux Cave is opened to the public.

The bulls in the Bull Gallery are probably the most famous masterpieces of the Lascaux Cave drawings.

Important Features

The Lascaux Cave is the most famous cave of the Vézère Valley and the most important rock art site in France. Its walls are decorated with paintings of lifelike animals, including bulls and mammoths. These are animals the people of Lascaux liked to hunt. They are painted in rich colors on the creamy white limestone cave walls.

Did You Know?
There is a painting of a unicorn in the Lascaux Cave.

Issues

The Lascaux Cave was closed to the public in 1963 because the air from the breath of so many visitors had begun to damage the fragile paintings. A visitor center was opened in 1983 with a **replica** cave and replica paintings for visitors to view.

GLOSSARY

prehistoric   from the time before writing was invented
replica   an exact copy

Index